They Say I Come From Hollywood Royalty . . . So Where's My Crown? is a memoir. All stories are retold to the best of the author's recollection.

Cover photos from William Wellman's personal files: Wellman Brentwood Farm; Cissy Wellman (age 7) on the set of *Across the Wide Missouri* with Clark Gable (and John Hodiak in the background).

ISBN: 979-8-695007-72-5

They Say I Come From Hollywood Royalty ...

So Where's My Crown?

Cissy Wellman

Contents

Introduction

Okay, so what's the question? Besides, So Where's My Crown?

The question is why am I writing this book? And that's a good question! I don't know!

I guess my answer is . . . why not?

I've done several talk shows and panels where I've been interviewed about my career and my dad's career, and after telling some of my stories, everybody says you've got such interesting and fun Hollywood stories, why don't you write them down, write a book?

So that's the answer to why I'm writing this book! I hope you have some fun reading my stories.

On our Brentwood farm in 1950.
Cissy, Tim, Kitty, Billy, Pat, Mom, Dad, and Mikey
(Maggie arrives one year later)

Dad and Me

I'm Cissy Wellman, daughter of pioneer film director William Wellman. Some films he directed were *Wings*, which won the first Academy Award in 1927 for best film, the original *Star is Born* that he wrote and directed and won the Academy Award for writing, *Public Enemy, Nothing Sacred, GI Joe, Battleground, The Ox-Bow Incident, Roxie Hart, Beau Geste, The High and the Mighty*, to name a few.

Dad was thirty-seven when he married my nineteen-year-old mom, so he was forty-four when I was born. I was the fifth child of seven: Pat, Billy, Kitty, Tim, Cissy, Mike, and Maggie.

I'm the middle child. When I was the youngest it was great—I got the attention. Then came Mike and Maggie, and I didn't get the attention I was used to, being the younger of the five. By the time I was nine, I was too young to do things with the older ones and too old to do anything with the younger ones, so I didn't feel "a part of." I didn't fit in. When the entire family was together during vacations and holidays, that was fabulous. But as I got older the family dynamics changed. At least that's when I began to notice favoritism.

My father holding me as a baby.

Dad's favorite was my sister Kitty. She was beautiful, born pretty. I was a funny looking, freckle-faced redhead with buck teeth, and was labeled the good-natured one in the family. I was constantly told I shouldn't feel sad or angry because I was good natured.

I changed as the years went by. I got braces and started to become an attractive adult. I remember when I was eighteen and danced on *The Andy Williams Show* on TV. During a rty at the house my dad pulled me into the bar and said, "You know, it's amazing but you've become the beauty of the family with your looks, hair, coloring. You walk into a room and all eyes are on you, then you open your mouth and f*** it up."

One time I asked him, "Do you love me at all?"

He said, "Of course I love you, in my own way. I'm just a cantankerous old son of a b****." That sums up my relationship with my dad.

I found out years later that one of the reasons we didn't get along was because he saw things in me he didn't like in himself. Today I realize that they are really okay in me. It took a lot of working on myself to realize that. Working on the twelve steps in AA helped me to realize it—especially the fourth and fifth steps. The fourth step involves making a searching and fearless moral inventory of ourselves and the fifth step says we admitted to God, to ourselves, and to another human being the exact nature of our wrongs.

Dad and I did have good times together. I loved sitting and listening to him play the piano, listening to him read parts of his writings, walking the grounds of our home where he'd tell me stories. We lived on four acres in Brentwood— really a farm with horses, chickens, an orange orchard, pool, sports court, game room.

When Donner and I were buying our first and only home together, I asked Dad what we should do because we had two houses we liked. One was on Valley Vista in Sherman Oaks, California, for $62,000 and the other was on Longview Valley

Road south of Ventura Boulevard, also in Sherman Oaks, fc $35,000. Now this was the early '70s. Dad told me, "Neve let the house own you, own the house!" And then he asked, "Do you know how much I paid for our home? Four acres in Brentwood, bought in 1939—$27,500! Paid all cash directing three films!"

Yes, these were special times that I will always remember and say thank you, Dad, I love you.

Oh, we bought the Longview Valley Road home!

Aerial view of the Brentwood farm in the 2000s.

Richard and Robert

When I met Richard Donner (producer/director of blockbuster films such as *Superman* and *Lethal Weapon 1, 2,* and *3*), I was twenty and he was just starting to be known.

He saved my life. That might sound a little dramatic, but it is the truth.

When I was fifty-five years old, I got a letter from the Screen Actors Guild telling me that my health coverage would end in two years. I was on "self-pay" and thought that I had health coverage forever.

Surprise . . . not to happen. The letter said I had to earn $7,500 as an actor in one year to qualify, which meant I had two years to make $7,500!

So I called everybody I knew for help.

At the time I was in real estate, and doing very well, so I called Clint Eastwood. He was a friend and I had done two movies with him—*Play Misty For Me* and *Outlaw Josey Wales*. In addition, my ex-husband Robert Donner was a dear friend of his. I left Clint a message and said "Please help me Clint, edit me out of whatever you're doing. I'll pay you back," and explained why I needed the job and the earnings. My husband at the time, Greg Guydus, was a diabetic with rheumatoid arthritis and if we didn't have the SAG health-care we probably would be on the streets and have to sell our home, everything. The cost of his hospitalization, surgeries, and medication was astronomical without insurance. I never heard back from Clint.

One person who did help me out the first year was dear sweet Jeffrey Kramer. Jeffrey was a good friend. I got to know Jeffrey and Vikki, his wife at the time, through Judy Farrell and her husband Joe Bratcher. I helped Jeffrey and Vikki buy their first home and then when they separated I helped them both—Jeffrey buying his new home and Vikki selling and then buying her condo. It was a special relationship because they trusted me, in other words neither knew what the other was doing, at least not from me. I wouldn't take sides! Jeffrey had me do some voice-overs for his shows. I also did an *Ally McBeal* for him.

Penny Perry was another friend who cast me in some Lifetime movies. (In 2015 Penny cast me in a wonderful Hallmark movie *Portrait of Love* in which I co-starred, a really wonderful role. Thank you Penny.) But this was still not enough to make $7,500. I think I made about $3,500 the first year and the second year was coming—this was it. If I didn't make the $7,500 it was going to be . . . well, I can't even imagine what it would have been like. And if I make the $7,500, then the next year I wouldn't have to pay monthly deductions for my insurance and the year after that, I would start "self pay" again for eight years until I turn sixty-five.

So, I had about seven months left and I'd only made $2,500. Ten years without any insurance with all that my poor husband had to go through, such as surgeries and amputations—we wouldn't be able to exist unless we sold our house.

So, as a last resort I called Richard Donner, who I hadn't seen in at least forty years!

How did we know each other? When I was twenty years old, I was going with Robert Donner and engaged to marry Robert Donner. *Variety* and *Hollywood Reporter* (show biz papers) reported news to the effect that director William Wellman's actress daughter, Cissy Wellman, was engaged to actor Robert Donner.

People started saying to me, "Oh, you're marrying Richard Donner," and I'd say, "No, who's Richard Donner?" This kept happening for months.

"You're marrying Richard Donner?"

"No, what's a Richard Donner? Is he related to Richard Donner? No!"

When Robert and I got married in December, my friends

and acquaintances congratulated me on marrying Richard Donner! And I had to keep saying, "No! It's *Robert* Donner, not related to *Richard* Donner!"

Well, my new husband and I were at a Christmas party and I was sitting on a couch when all of a sudden this finger tapped me on the shoulder from behind. I turned around and there was this very attractive man. He said, "Hi, I just want to say I really enjoy being married to you. My name is Richard Donner."

Well, we laughed, and I asked, "Oh, my God, you're getting the same thing from everybody?"

"Yes," he said. "I kept getting congratulations from everyone on being engaged to Cissy Wellman, Bill Wellman's daughter, and then I got congratulated on marrying Cissy Wellman, Bill Wellman's daughter. I kept saying who's Cissy Wellman?"

Needless to say we had a few laughs over this.

Richard and I had never worked together, but we kept running into each other over the years. He was, and is still, one of the most generous, selfless men I know. We did some charity events together. We helped raise money for James Stacy when he had his motorcycle accident and lost his leg and his arm. We never worked together because I had pretty much stopped working when I married Robert Donner. I started really running his career (that's another story).

So, now I called Richard Donner. His secretary told me

.e was out of the country, and I said of course he is and
. added, "Would you please leave him a message that the
the other Mrs. Donner, Cissy Wellman called?"

Within a half hour he called me back and he was laugh-
.ng. He said his secretary only gave him the message that the
ex other Mrs. Donner called, and said the name Cissy Wellman and then he called me.

When I told him my story, his response was, "Why didn't
you call me when I was doing *Lethal Weapon 3*?"

I said, "Dick, do you realize how hard it is for me to make
this call?"

"Don't worry, it's taken care of," he said.

Even though he was out of the country, he called Joel
Silver—another big producer at Warner Brothers where
Richard's office was located. He called me back and said that
Joel had nothing going on, but "Don't worry I'm going to get
you with my assistant. Just give him a picture and resume
and something will work out."

Within two months I got a call from his assistant who
told me they had a movie that they were producing for HBO
called *Made Men* starring Jim Belushi and directed by Louis
Morneau from Canada, and there were only three women
roles in the film. Two of them I wasn't right for—they were
young. The third one was supposed to be an eighty-year-old
character like Ma Kettle. If the director bought me as the
old lady, it was mine! Remember I'm fifty-five at the time.

I read the script and it was a wonderful role. Frances was
the character's name, and she had a sixteen-page scene that

was just wonderful! I'm with the casting director and to. my story and read for her. I put on a gray wig and, of cou no makeup and she told me to "bring it down a little b when I met with the director and read for him.

So, I go in and I meet the director and he's filming me. When I finished he said, "Can you have more fun with her?" The casting director immediately piped in. "Boy, can she! I was the one that told her to bring it down!"

So I did it again. After I finished, the director said, "Are we going to have fun! Lose the wig, just put the hair back in a bun and we'll do makeup to age you!" Yipeeee!

This was probably one of my favorite roles to play. I knew what I wanted to do with Frances. I was a size eight. I'm about a ten now but when the wardrobe lady called me and we talked about what Frances was going to wear, she asked me my size, and I said fourteen. When she brought the clothes over, I had just been to a luncheon and was dressed up. She took one look at me as I answered the door and said, "Is your mother here?" I fell in love with her immediately. I said, "No, it's me," and she started laughing.

"Oh, my God, I wish all my actresses were like you," she said. Nice compliment.

After all these years of not acting and getting this role, well, I realized that I had self confidence. I was good, and my ego was left at the door. Twelve years of sobriety, doing the twelve steps had paid off. I no longer felt "lesser than" or not enough. What a breakthrough—I could breathe! And thank a higher power.

❀

had fun because the character Frances had no body. She
~n a little market in a nowhere place. I had her wearing a
~oose dress with a loose apron, and the slip falling off her
shoulder, and rumpled socks with her shoes.

When I got to the location, the assistant director took me
to my dressing room and when we opened the door I saw
placed on the bed my clothes plus some bras. I just looked
at the assistant director and said, "Oh no . . . Frances doesn't
wear bras. Her tits have fallen and she doesn't care." The assistant director really laughed and said, "Boy are you going to fit
in here." This was 1998, and I was only in Utah shooting one
day with two days of travel, and it's scale which meant at that
time I only made $1,500. I needed to make $5,000.

When I was finished shooting, my paycheck arrived—
and it was for the $5,000!

Richard Donner would not let me pay it back. So you
see—he saved my life.

I came up with a gift for him that I thought he'd really like
because he loves showbiz and old Hollywood. I have a picture of myself sitting on Clark Gable's lap when I was seven
years old, with John Hodiak (he played a Native American)
in the background.

This was during the shooting of *Across the Wide Missouri*
which my father directed, and as a kid I remember it vividly.
It was 1950 and they filmed in Durango, Colorado. Mom and
six of us Wellman kids (my sister Maggie wasn't born yet)

were there for the summer. We fished in the stream, swam in the pool, and Clark Gable was really nice. He was married to Lady Ashley at the time and the one thing I remember was Gable walking his two dogs. I remember this because the dogs are not the breed I would picture Clark Gable having— two chihuahuas! Maybe two huskies, but not chihuahuas! I blew the photo up into poster size, framed it and signed it, "To Richard, We thank you from the bottom of our hearts! Clark, John and Cissy."

His secretary told me that when he received it he was so excited he put it up on the wall immediately.

You don't hear enough good Hollywood stories. That's a shame, because there are some wonderful people there, like Richard Donner who helped when I was in need. Thank you sweet Richard.

Durango, Colorado. 1950.

Visiting Dad on the set of *Across the Wide Missouri*.

From left to right: Billy, me, Pat, Mom, Tim, and Kitty. Dad is holding Mike.

Mom

My mother, Dorothy Coonan, was one of the original Busby Berkeley dancers. She started dancing professionally when she was fifteen. She was in *42nd Street*, *Kid from Spain*, *Gold Diggers of 33*, amongst others.

Mom acted and danced with Frankie Darrow in *Wild Boys of the Road* which Dad directed in 1933. (Mom only acted in two movies, both directed by Dad. The other was *The Story of G.I. Joe*.)

She was one of six children. She married my dad
she was nineteen and he was thirty-seven. My mother wa
fifth wife and they had seven children. They had an amaz
forty-two year relationship, especially the early years befo.
Dad got older and retired. In their early years, they rode
motorcycles together. They had a motorcycle group that was
called The Moraga Spit and Polish Club, which consisted of
Mom, Dad, Victor Fleming, Howard and Slim Hawks, Andy
and Doggie Devine, Keenan Wynn, Robert Taylor, and Barbara Stanwyck, just to name a few.

Holy moly! What an amazing group and an amazing
time! Mom and Dad played golf together, fished together,
and were really good friends. I don't think I ever heard them
fight, except about how many strokes he was going to give
her in golf.

Dad had it in his contract that when he was shooting in
town he would "wrap early" so he could be home in time for
six pm dinner with the family. Mother was the cook. She was
a really good cook and she cooked healthily. We had vegeta-
ble gardens. Did I mention we lived on a four-plus acre farm
and in Brentwood!?

Mom was also an amazing seamstress and made a lot of
her own clothes. She even made some of our prom dresses,
bathing suits, and tennis dresses. That's how I learned to
sew bathing suits and tennis dresses. They were also fun and
easy to do.

Dad really worshiped the ground Mom walked on. Everything was about Mom. At the dinner table, God forbid if

er happened to be sick upstairs in her room. He would sit there, growl and say, "Wait on your mother! I don't e a damn about you kids, it's your mother I care about!" eirdly, we found it quite loving.

Dad did have a temper though. When he got mad he was rather scary, to say the least. He'd be real quiet but his face would change and his ears would go back. Needless to say you could tell he was not a happy camper! God forbid you asked a question or said anything like "pass the butter." He would just start in on you and you were it! And I was "it" a lot of the time!

Mom really wasn't emotional or very demonstrative, at least with me. She was basically a quiet person. I was like Dad—not very quiet. I think that was a trait in me she didn't like, but she put up with it in Dad. Mom and I would go to the movies, and if it was a comedy and I laughed a little too loud, she would shush me.

A lot of times I felt as though I had to walk on eggshells around her.

Some of the good times with Mom and me.

We grew up in the era of "Don't air dirty laundry." Fe[...]
were not expressed, unless they were happy ones. The s[...]
of us kids were all labeled. I was the good-natured one.
if, God forbid, I got a feeling that wasn't good natured,
would be told "You can't feel that way. Remember you're the
good-natured one in the family."

So I stuffed all my negative feelings, fearful feelings, any
feeling that wasn't a happy one. If it sounds like I didn't love
my mom, that's not true. Looking back now, I had the best
childhood you could ever ask for. She was an amazing and
beautiful woman. She also loved playing with us . . . kick the
can, hide n' seek, jump rope, tennis—and Dad loved watching us all.

I remember one time when she was in her seventies, I
called to see how she was doing and she said she sprained
her ankle.

"How?" I asked. She said she was playing kick the can
with some of the grandkids and was jumping off the wall!

She never swore, yet Dad did and a lot . . . sometimes
when he was swearing at someone on the phone, we couldn't
tell if he was mad or not! Most of the time it was his typical
greeting: "Why you old SOB! How the hell are you?"

Mom stood five feet, two inches tall, and always weighed
approximately 110 pounds, unless she was pregnant! She was
a moderate person. Never overate, only had a drink before
dinner and maybe a glass of wine with dinner. I wish I had
inherited that gene! She was the perfect definition of an elegant lady.

My beautiful mother.

Born to Act Players

Twelve years ago, in 2008, I was thinking of getting out of real estate, and going back to having fun. Showbiz! One of my last clients was a referral from Carolyne Barry, a great acting coach, dancer, and actress I loved very much and who has passed. She and I spent much time together in New York, working in commercials, having picnics in the park, just plain hanging together! Great times in New York! I go back on occasion to see plays and get my New York fix.

The client's name was David Zimmerman, who has become a good friend. David is creator and producer of *Meet The Biz* workshops, which look to make diversity commonplace and bridges the gap between ability and disability. He has one of the biggest hearts of anyone I've ever known. He and Mary Rings!

While we were looking for condos, I told him that he w
going to be my last client, that I wanted to go back to gettir
my creative fixes. I mentioned that I really wanted to wor.
with kids. He said, "Well, they're not really kids but I used to
work with a group called Born to Act Players—BTAPs. They
have Down Syndrome, autism and special abilities. Would
you be interested in going with me sometime to see them?"

A voice out of my mouth said, "Yes."

Which, I must admit, was sort of a surprise because I
think I had the general population feeling about Down Syndrome and autism. It was *no* knowledge. I had a fear of them,
of not knowing how to act around them. I didn't hear back
from David for about a month. So I really thought maybe it's
good that I don't have to go.

Then he called me one Monday, and said "I'm going to go
Saturday to the Born to Act Players. Do you want to come?"

Again I said "Yes!" Another surprise that *yes* came out of
my mouth!

It was the best thing I ever did. I walked into this group
and fell in love. They were rehearsing a musical. I found out
they put on two shows a year. As I was sitting watching, they
blew me away. Their love, passion, honesty, and talent just
knocked me out! I literally had tears of joy.

I met Mary Rings who started this group, now as of this
writing which is 2020, about 26 years ago. She started BTAP
with her son Casey who has Down Syndrome. She and David

merman, have the biggest hearts of anybody I've ever
own! You watch Mary with the group and the love is pal-
able. I don't think I've ever seen Mary without a smile on
her face! I've stayed with BTAP for over twelve years and I
must say, this has a lot to do with Mary. She is not a Diva. If
she were, I probably would have left immediately. How she
works with her students, her love, her patience just knocked
me out. We've become very good friends.

This group is my passion. If the world were more like
these people, what a wonderful place it would be. They're
honest, loving and they wear their hearts on their sleeves.
They tell you exactly what they're thinking, how they
feel. They get pissed and don't hold a resentment—what a
concept! Doing improvs, dancing and singing with them
weekly is a joy. It is amazing. They keep you on your toes.
They are so bright, so fast. They are a joy.

I've taken a little time off from BTAP as of this writing. It's
been about a year since I've been there. I had some health
issues to deal with so I needed to take a break. I will be back
though and any chance I get, I talk about BTAP. They are very
talented, very high functioning people. Anyone who wants to
know more about them just go on to *BorntoActPlayers.com*.
Come see our shows and support BTAP, it's a non-profit.

Mary's assistants are really quite wonderful. They are
all volunteers and I am one of them. We've had so many
wonderful guests come and play with us. I got Anna Gunn,

Michael Learned, Judy Norton Taylor, David Har
Judy Keel, and even Dick Gautier, who besides having be
a wonderful comedian actor, was an incredible artist. He d.
wonderful cartoons. He brought a huge pad of paper and
charcoals and did tons of drawings for the kids.

You notice I call them kids. Well, their ages are nineteen
to forty-five but hell, I'm seventy-seven, so they are kids to
me. I never had children. They became the kids I wish I had.

Everyone says what a great thing I do for them, but in
truth it's what they do for me. The joy that I get with them
is from watching how they change, how they become
more secure. They have helped me become more of a giving
person.

The Born to Act Players.
Director and creator, Mary Riggs, is in the white shirt in the center.

never forget when Brandon started with the group. He ould just sit, refusing to get up and play with us. I would go him and say, "Come on Brandon, come up on stage and play."

He would just shake his head and wag his finger *No*.

I said, "Come have fun with us, it's fun."

He would just shake his head again *No!*

So I asked him, "Why?"

"They'll laugh at me!"

"Brandon do you see them laughing at me when I'm up there on stage?" I asked him.

He nodded his head up and down, *Yes*.

I said, "If they don't laugh, that's when I get upset! It's really fun and nobody's laughing at you for the wrong reason." Since that time Brandon has sung in our shows. He gets up, does improvs, and he feels safe. It's an environment where everyone feels safe. It gets them to be comfortable out in the real world because they know they are perfect as they are.

Brandon
and me.

Then there's Robin Trocki. She was on *Glee*, playing J̣
Lynch's sister. She was so delicious to work with in impro
because you never knew where she was going. She kept yo
on your toes.

Robin and
me.

In one of the improvs, I had six of the Born to Act Players
in it. The format was "The best chef would win a million
dollars." Well, each had a stool in front of them, then we
started, everybody was at their stool except Robin who from
backstage started coming down stage pantomiming pulling
something downstage. So I asked, "Chef Robin, what are you
doing?"

"I'm pulling my turkey!" she said.

"Is your turkey still alive?" I asked.

She said, "No, my turkey is dead. I need to stuff my

turkey!" All with a slight New York accent and then she pantomimed lifting up the turkey and putting it on the stool.

I asked "What are you going to stuff your turkey with, Chef Robin?"

With that she pantomimed putting her head in the turkey and said, "I'm stuffing the turkey with my head!" So hard to keep from laughing!

I turned my attention to each of the other actors to find out what they were doing with their meals. Then I'd look and there was Robin still with her head in the turkey!

So I said to Robin, "Chef Robin, how is it going with your turkey?"

"I'm still stuffing the turkey with my head," she said. "It will be ready soon!" It was really hard not to crack up. I loved Robin Trocki. I was able to spend time with her because I drove her to and from class a lot of the time. She developed Alzheimer's and has passed. My heart goes out to her sweet sister, Sharon, who has become a dear friend. We still talk often and have lunch on occasion.

I really love every one of the Born to Act Players. Being with them has been such a wonderful gift. If I never get paid to act again and just get to work with my BTAPs, I'm really a very happy camper. I will be back with them soon!! I miss their hugs and love!

Yancy Tucker (My husband Robert Donner)
and Sissy Walker (me) on *The Waltons*.

The Waltons

A lot of people ask me how I got on *The Waltons*. Well, I did it by sleeping with the actor, who I happened to be married to—Robert Donner.

He was playing the character Yancy Tucker on the show. Earl Hamner, the creator, was one of the most gentle men I have ever met. When you hear the word gentleman, if you want a perfect description, it's Earl Hamner. His wife Jane is a true lady!

Earl came to me one day and asked if I'd like to visit my husband in jail? I said that sounds like fun. So he wrote the character, Jane Aspen, to visit Yancy in jail. I believe it was the next season that Earl came to me and asked if I'd like to play Yancy's girlfriend or soon-to-be girlfriend as a recurring role? Donner and I looked at each other and said that'll work.

Another picture of Robert Donner and me on *The Waltons*.

I was blessed to have done the show for five seasons, from 1973 to 1978. I guested on six shows and I must say, it was one of the best experiences I've ever had, especially getting to know the cast. It was really a great group. Judy Norton Taylor, who played the oldest daughter Mary Ellen on *The Waltons*, happens to be a major talent. She acts, writes, directs, produces and sings like nobody's business. She is so good.

We have kept in touch. Anytime she's doing a cabaret act, I'm there. She even asked me to do a role in her web

. I played her friend and agent. It was a joy working
. her.

I visited Earl at his office on Ventura Boulevard in Stu-
.io City on numerous occasions. He had many fishes on the
walls, well actually everywhere, so I gave him a mechanical
singing fish that he could mount on the wall, and he laughed.
Any time I think of Earl, I smile.

Thank you, Earl, for being you.

These days, I see Michael Learned, who played the mother,
Olivia, on *The Waltons*, quite often. She's a dynamite woman
and a very funny and talented lady. I get to see a lot of the cast
on the reunions, when I'm asked to join them. The fans of
The Waltons, oh my, they are the best. They're so loving and
special. Every time I've gone back to Virginia or Missouri for
a reunion, the fans are warm and welcoming, never intrusive
at all.

On the fortieth anniversary reunion back in Virginia,
2013, I had the pleasure of meeting two very tall, gorgeous,
incredible women. They were in the bookstore looking at
some Walton paraphernalia. I didn't recognize them from
the people I'd seen there so far, and trust me there were a lot
of people, more than 300. So, I went up to them and saw that
they were looking at some of the Waltons books. They spoke
in German, even though I didn't speak German, I still was
bold enough to ask them if they were fans of *The Waltons*.
The mother said yes.

I said, "Well, this happens to be your lucky day b
Jim Bob is right over there." That was David Harper.

She looked at me and said, "You were on the show a
weren't you?"

"Yes, I played Sissy Walker who worked at the Dew Drop
Inn and married Yancy Tucker." Then I asked them if they
were there for the reunion.

She said no, they didn't know anything about it. "How
did you become fans of *The Waltons*?"

"In Germany we do have a television but we don't have
any cable," she explained. "We only watch DVDs, and when
my daughter, Josephine, was thirteen, she brought home the
first season of *The Waltons* and we fell in love with it and
proceeded to watch all the other seasons for the next few
years." After watching all the seasons they decided that when
they came to the United States they would go to Walton's
Mountain.

Wow, what a coincidence!!

When I met Josephine
and Jutta at *The
Waltons* reunion in
Virginia in 2013.

ell, I took them under my wing, I got them to come us to the original Earl Hamner Walton house. They had ch with us. I got them into the Fan Club Dinner. I fell in ve with Jutta and Josephine Smith. They are now members of *The Waltons* fan club on FaceBook!

Just a few years ago, in 2015, Jutta and her friend Linda Achtert came to the United States mainly to see Lionel Richie in Vegas. Jutta is a major fan of Lionel Richie. They stayed with me for two days, and I was their tour guide! I took them around and showed them everywhere. I was a great tour guide plus it was fun.

I had a great surprise for them. I took them to the Beverly Hills Hotel Polo Lounge for lunch and unbeknownst to them, I got Michael Learned, who wasn't at the reunion, and Linda Purl, who was also on *The Waltons* and a friend of mine, to join us. I met Linda Purl shooting the series *The Young Pioneers*, which my then-husband Robert Donner was also in, and we remained friends. I helped her buy two of her houses and sell them. Any time she sings at any venue I'm there. This lady has a voice to die for!

Well getting back to the Polo Lounge, Jutta and Linda were so surprised and excited to meet Michael and Linda— they just loved it! Then, guess who walks in? Lionel Richie! Oh my God, the two of them were absolutely beside themselves. Well, sweet Ms. Michael went back to Lionel Richie's table, told them about Jutta and her friend coming all the way from Germany just to see him in Vegas. He invited us all back to his table and he talked to all of us, mainly with them.

He was so welcoming, friendly, and warm. It was re
very special. Just watching the girls—they were crying!
they just touched my heart. It's an experience I will ne
forget.

Life is so interesting—it was a major God shot! Here they
are in Beverly Hills on their way to Vegas to see their favorite
singer and he drops into the Beverly Hills Hotel the same
time they're there . . . serendipitous.

Some of *The Waltons* cast as adults helping at a fundraiser for the Will
Geer Theatricum Botanicum in Topanga Canyon.

Richard Thomas

All of *The Waltons* kids are such wonderful people, and so talented. I was so very lucky to have been a part of that show and to be on a set that was so loving and to have met these wonderful people.

There was one show I did with Richard Thomas, one of his last shows. It was the episode where Merle Haggard was the other guest star. My character was trying to make Yancy jealous, so I was flirting with John Boy. One scene we were shooting on the set was in a car. I was driving John Boy and was very flirtatious.

My line was, "So how does a young man like you find all the time to do all that you do? My, my, do you have time for anything other than work . . . ?" and more like that.

When we finished rehearsing the director said, "Cissy,

this is an old car you have to shift." I said to the director, Harvey Laidman, "Harvey, if my hand leaves the camera frame it's going to look like I'm grabbing for his crotch the way this scene is playing!" Everybody laughed.

So, when we did the take, I went to shift, and Richard Thomas gave a little "Oops!" sound and sort of bounced up like I had grabbed his crotch. Of course I cracked up, as did everybody else. He did that for a couple of more takes until we finally did it right but it was so much fun, and of course, the scene did not end up in the show. Richard was a joy to work with.

Speaking of Richard Thomas: Yes I have been on Broadway! It was 1978 and I was back in New York working at doing commercials. Richard was starring in the *Fifth of July* along with Swoozie Kurtz and Mary Carver on Broadway. I called Richard to let him know I was there and he got me four house seats for the show so I invited my close friend Arlene Golonka and Darren McGavin and his wife Cathy.

Well, there's a scene where the actor playing Richard Thomas's brother asks Richard's character if there are any phone messages for him and Richard read off several phone messages and he said one was from "Sissy from the Dew Drop Inn"! Yes that was the character I played on *The Waltons* with Richard. We all giggled.

So thank you, Richard Thomas, I can now say I've been on Broadway!

Welcoming the New Person

When it came to the part of the show where Yancy and Sissy get married, the last scene was our going to bed and turning out the lights. At this point we started saying, "Goodnight Earl, goodnight John Boy, good night Ralph . . ." We went through the entire cast names like they always do at the end of each show. We got a few chuckles to say the least.

It was a very warm, special show to do. I always made it a point to go up and introduce myself to a new actor to the show and say, "Welcome to the show." That's very important because it's really hard to be a newcomer, to not feel like "a part of." So just somebody saying "Welcome" can really make everything so much easier.

In point of fact, I was visiting a friend of mine, Da.
Gladstone, a really good actor and writer, when he was gues.
ing on *Simon & Simon* starring Gerald McRaney. While I was
standing talking to Dana, all of a sudden Gerald comes over.
I didn't think I knew him, only by his work, which I really
liked a lot.

He said, "You're Cissy Wellman."

I said, "Yes . . ."

"I just want to thank you," he said. "I had a small part
on *The Waltons* and you came to me and said 'Welcome.' I'll
never forget that."

It's amazing who you can touch by just being a little
warmer, friendlier human being.

Some of My Crazy Casting Stories

In 1977 I was cast as the guest star on *Charlie's Angels*. It was the very first show where Cheryl Ladd replaced Farrah as an Angel. My then-husband Robert Donner and I were friends with David Doyle and his beautiful wife Anne. David was Bosley on *Charlie's Angels* and David and I were in a singing class together.

In David Craig's fabulous singing workshop, he worked with actors to get them to sing. In addition to being a singing coach he was probably one of the best acting coaches. In his class to do a number you had to write a subtext for it and sing the subtext.

It was a fabulous class and one Sunday, David and Anne

had an outdoor tea party at their house and asked all the guests to dress for high tea. David hired live musicians to play and people would get up and sing. Well, when David asked me to sing, I sang "On a Clear Day." I was dressed to the nines—I looked FABULOUS, if I say so myself!

The next day my agent called me and said you just booked the guest star on *Charlie's Angels*. I said you mean I have to go and read for it? He said, no, we booked it, you got it!

Wow! That's nice!

When I got to the set, the director was Paul Stanley who was at David Doyle's tea party. I asked him how I got cast and he said he was talking to the producers about who to get for the lead. He said, what about Cissy Wellman? And they said, who's Cissy Wellman? He replied she's a good actress and she sang "On a Clear Day" yesterday at David's tea party.

And they said perfect, cast her!

So you never know!

Then there was *Hart to Hart* in 1979. I had been mainly working on *The Waltons* during this time. When it came out that the next show of *Hart to Hart* was about redheaded hookers being killed off, I said to my agent, get me a reading, I'm a redhead!

Well, he said they wouldn't see me because I only do *The Waltons*. So ridiculous. But luckily the director was Ralph Senensky who had directed me on *The Waltons* so I called him and said Ralph, please let me come in and read for you ecause the casting people won't bring me into read for it. So he called me in, I read for it and I got it. I loved playing a hooker!

Thank you, Ralph.

Ralph Senensky directing me in *Hart to Hart.*

In 1979 I read for the guest star role on *Chips* and when I was there waiting to go in to read for the director and producers I saw the other three actresses who were also reading for it. I knew them and they were good actresses, so when I got the part again on the set, I asked the director Barry Crane, why me? He said all of you were great but you were the only one who had never done *Chips*! Who knew?

Thank you, Barry Crane. Crazy business! You can't take things personally. It's hard to do but it's the only way to survive!

Elvis

I met Elvis Presley in 1959 when I was sixteen years old. My brother Bill was dating an actress named Joan Staley, and when Bill was away in the National Guard one Saturday, Joan came by the house and asked me if I wanted to go with her to the beach. So I got in her car and we drove to the beach.

She impressed me with a lot of the people who she knew.

She said "Elvis has a house right there on Pacific Coast Highway. Let's drop in and see him." She said she was friends with him. I had to get back into town because I was going on a date with my then-boyfriend Bob Rhem. But OH, MY GOD—Elvis Presley! Well, we stopped by but nobody was there. Then just as we were pulling out, in came three cars, one of which contained Elvis Presley.

He stepped out of the car and there he was, in person.

Elvis Presley, oh my God, oh my God, Elvis oh, my God, oh my God, oh my God, oh my God!

Yes, he was gorgeous in person, and yes, I was nervous and excited! Well, they asked us to come in and so we did. Elvis was so nice and so were his guys. Elvis sat me down and asked me a lot of questions about myself. He just took an interest in me, and believe me, I was a bit nervous to say the least.

It was really a very special couple of hours getting to be with Elvis Presley. He asked if we wanted to stay there and have dinner. It didn't happen—I had to get back in town for my date, but I must say, I really wished I didn't have a date to go back to.

In 1961 when I was eighteen, I got to visit the Paramount Studio lot and at the time Howard Hawks was directing *Hatari* with John Wayne, Red Buttons and Elsa Martinelli. Frank Capra was directing *Pocketful of Miracles* with Glenn Ford, Hope Lange, Peter Falk, and Betty Davis. Elvis was doing *Blue Hawaii*. Well, I had access to all the sets so I just gritted my teeth and got my nerve up and went on to the set of *Blue Hawaii* to reintroduce myself to Elvis.

He remembered me and we became friends. He used to call me Freckles and I used to hang with him and the guys and play touch football. I was invited to some of his parties and went. One time he said to me, "Hey Freckles, you know you're one of the guys now so just don't get around me if I'm drinking 'cause I may have to turn queer."

Yes he was fun and funny. This was in the beginning of

his success and he was slender and happy and just a super-easy, wonderful down-to-earth guy. I was so lucky to be able to go on all those sets and I did visit those sets daily for weeks. I love being on sets, watching, learning and sometimes I was lucky enough to be working. You might say I was a "set groupie!" I still am!

Pickleball

It was May 23, 2018, and I had just gotten back from a weekend in Santa Barbara. I was there because my beautiful brother Mikey and his wife Suzy from Kauai flew here, first to San Francisco to visit his daughter Molly, and then came down to spend time with his sons Kyle, his wife, Kristy and kids, and Matty and his wife, Shay. Then on to Santa Barbara where my sister Maggie and her husband, Dan, came down from Ojai.

They were all playing in a pickleball tournament! I was there to support. Well, I had so much fun. It's a tough game, a fun game. Watching it was very stressful—I felt like I was working out with them! I must say when I got home after three days of walking, watching, being with them, I was exhausted. It's amazing—my mind says I'm nineteen and my

body says, don't think so! I had to rest for two days to fe
close to normal, only close. Aging is very interesting. But I do
look forward to learning how to play Pickleball. I don't want
to play in tournaments though—I'm not that competitive—
but I would like to do it to have fun. My body might be able
to keep up, and then again . . .

My beautiful little sister Maggie visiting me
on the set of *Red Line 7000*.

A Howard Hawks Story

(of which there will be many)

Howard was like the father I wish my dad had been. In case you're not familiar with him, he directed such films as *To Have and Have Not*, *Red River*, *Gentlemen Prefer Blondes*, *The Big Sleep*, *Bringing Up Baby*, *Sergeant York* and *Rio Bravo*.

Howard accepted me for me, loved me for me, and I loved him. He had a great sense of humor. Now, in case you've never met me, I'm five-foot-three, red-headed, and at the time I weighed 116 pounds. Howard was tall, six-feet, two inches, and lean. He loved tall lean brunette actresses a la Lauren Bacall. There was one time on the set of *Red Line 7000*, in 1964, that I walked up and asked him if I was really

a tall lean brunette and was fooling myself all these year
He grinned and said, "Nope," then did his funny little giggle
I jumped up, kissed him on the cheek turned and sashayed
away.

Howard had me stage the dance number in *Red Line
7000*. The two actresses he had who he wanted in the dance
number with Carol Conors and me . . . well, unfortunately
they couldn't dance. So I said, "Howard, these two ladies can't
dance and they're the first to admit it, so unless you want me
to do a class to teach actresses how to dance it's not going to
work."

So he said, "Fire them and hire two dancers you want to
work with." Oh my God, I didn't want to fire anybody, no way.
So he did it. I was able to hire Teri Garr and Roberta Tennis,
two ladies who I really loved, and I loved their dancing. As a
matter of fact, Teri and I had danced in a Crest commercial
together. I was the one who was the better dancer and she was
the one who had the better teeth. The truth is, it's absolutely
the opposite in real life—Teri is the much better dancer and
I have the better teeth. This was at the time when Teri was
mainly dancing and getting her acting career started. So I
told Howard that they had to be hired as actresses, not extras,
so they would get paid more. Teri was so funny that I used to
try to get Howard to come over and watch her. He proceeded
to give her lines and she ended up with a nice little part.

In my opinion Teri Garr is one of the funniest actresses
we have ever had.

❀

Howard and I spent a lot of time together. He lived in Palm Springs and I used to visit him a lot, and spend days and weekends with him, especially when my husband Robert Donner was on location.

One time I spent time with him was right before the James Franciscus Celebrity Tennis Tournament, in which I was playing with my husband Robert. Unfortunately Robert couldn't join us until the tournament started, so I went down early to be with Howard.

Well, what they do at this tournament is they have a Calcutta—people bid on the teams. Howard joined us that night for the party and the Calcutta. My mom was there with my brother Bill, his wife Flossie, as well as my sister Maggie and her then-husband Bill Driscoll, and of course my sister Kitty who was married to James Franciscus at the time.

When it came to the Cissy and Robert team, Howard Hawks started bidding on us. Interestingly enough, Mother had bought ALL the family teams all the years before—my brother Bill and his wife, and they won; my sister Kitty and James Franciscus, and they won; Maggie and Bill Driscoll, and they won! So it was her turn to buy us—at least that's what she thought! Well, Howard was making it very difficult for her. I mean it was really embarrassing and yet very satisfying. Mom and Howard kept bidding against each other, higher and higher, to buy us! Howard finally declined and let Mom buy us! And yes, we won!

❀

I loved Howard. His own daughter, Kitty, had the same kind of relationship with him that I had with my dad and I'm sorry she wasn't able to find a surrogate dad like I did in her father Howard.

When Howard passed it was 1977, it was two years after my dad died. I didn't want to go to the memorial service. I don't like them. But Howard's daughter, Barbara, called me and said, "Please come."

"I just don't want to wear black, it's not how I feel about Howard," I told her.

"I'm not wearing black—I'm wearing one of Dad's favorite dresses that's red," she said.

"That I can do," I said. "I have a fabulous rust colored dress and rust suede coat that Howard loved on me." So I wore it. While I was standing in the courtyard at the Episcopal Church in Beverly Hills, up walks John Wayne—"Duke."

He looked at me and said, "First it was John Ford, then your dad, now Howard. I've got no one left to bury." We went into each other's arms.

I loved that man, the DUKE. We never talked politics, but being on three films with him for approximately sixteen weeks each, I got to know him and like him a lot. He was very funny. we used to swim together. In one film called *Chisholm* I was staging the dance numbers. The director was Andrew

McLaglen, who used to be my father's assistant director. I introduced dear Donner, my husband, to Andrew. Andrew really liked Donner, as a person and as an actor. He used Donner in a lot of films, starting with *The Undefeated* and then of course *Chisholm*. I staged the dance numbers in those films.

Pat, Kitty, and I met John Wayne when we visited the set of *Island in the Sky* which Dad directed in 1953.

On *Chisolm*, I mentioned to McLaglen that a lot of the wives of the actors were complaining that their husbands just sit around on the set all day, and then when they come home they're tired! I said, let's put them to work so they can be in the dance numbers. We had the wardrobe—let them get to see what it's really like being on a set!

Andrew agreed. One of them was married to the cinematographer Bill Clothier, who had also been my dad's cinematographer. Carmen, had been here most of her life yet still had the thickest French accent. Duke wasn't particularly a fan of hers. The day I was blocking the dance number, Carmen came up and started to tell me how I should do it. The Duke observed this encounter. At the lunch break, he called me into his trailer. He started to do an imitation of Carmen. It was hysterical—he was dancing and flitting around the trailer. Needless to say, I ignored her suggestions because it was between me and the director. But it was the best thing I ever did for the actors because their wives never complained again. They realized how exhausting it is being on a set, sitting in between takes and sitting and sitting and sitting ...

I was blessed to have staged the dances in *The Undefeated* with John Wayne, Rock Hudson, Merlin Olsen, and Roman Gabriel. I fell in love with all of them, especially Merlin and Roman, my being a Rams fan. Rock Hudson was the sweetest man to be around. He was so enthusiastic. I don't think I ever saw him get upset with anything or anyone. Sometimes on location when we'd be having lunch, fans would come up while Rock was eating, stick paper in front of him and say, "Sign this," not *please* sign this, just an order to "Sign this."

He would very politely sign it!

Choreographing Merlin Olsen in *The Undefeated*. To my left are director Andrew McLaglen and Rock Hudson. The dancing children on the right are Andrew's son Josh and daughter Mary.

Rock also told funny stories about himself and his career. After that film was finished, we were invited to Rock's house on many occasions to have dinner and watch movies. I asked him questions about his films, especially *Giant* which I loved. He told me that George Stevens, the director, would take him around the set and ask him his advice on colors for the interiors of the set, what kind of furniture he wanted, made him a real part of the planning of the film.

There is one scene in the film where he and his wife, played by Elizabeth Taylor, had separated—she had gone back to her old home for her sister's wedding and unbeknownst to her, Rock Hudson came to the wedding. When she feels that he's there, she turns and looks at him . . . it was so touching that the wardrobe and makeup women were sobbing!

He told us the truth was that the night before was the first time he and Elizabeth had met. They got drunk together getting to know each other and were completely hung over during the shooting of that scene. Amazing.

By the way, he loved Elizabeth Taylor and they remained good friends.

Another Howard Hawks Story

During one of my many weekend visits with Howard, we decided to have a dinner party. He and I would cook. We invited Frank Capra who also lived down in Palm Springs with his wife Lucille, who I grew up with, and were good friends of my mom and dad's (the Capra family lived down the street from the Wellman family). Frank Capra won three Oscars and was nominated numerous times. His movies include *It's a Wonderful Life*, *It Happened One Night*, *Mr. Smith Goes to Washington*, and *Meet John Doe*.

Also invited that night were George and Terry Kirgo. George was a writer, a wonderful writer. He wrote *Red Line 7000* for Howard.

It was such a wonderful evening, Frank and Howard sharing stories back and forth. One would tell a story and it would remind the other one about another story. They just told such wonderful Hollywood stories.

George looked at me, said, "Damn, I sure wish we had a recording of this."

So do I, but at least I have the memory, and such a good one.

Yet Another Howard Hawks Story

One time when we were having lunch, Howard told me a story that I love to believe is true, especially since I love old Hollywood, having been raised in it.

Since he had done so many Humphrey Bogart and Lauren Bacall films, he was a little tired of doing them. He had just gotten another script that sounded like another Bacall-Bogart film. So, one day he was having lunch with the famous director Michael Curtiz—a few of his films are *White Christmas*, *Yankee Doodle Dandy* and *Angels with Dirty Faces*.

They were talking about how they each didn't like the stories they were going to do. Howard started telling Michael the story that he was going to do, and Michael told Howard

the story he was going to do. Each of them liked the ot
story so they decided to switch.

They each went back to their respective studios to see
they could switch. The studios said fine, switch!

Because of this, Howard Hawks directed *Sergeant York,*
of which he was nominated for an Academy Award, and
Michael Curtiz directed *Casablanca* for which he won an
Academy Award in 1941. Both classics—fun story!

Dinghy

This is a non-Hollywood story, except that it involves my husband at the time, Robert Donner and our incredible dog Dinghy, who got his name because he was a little crazy, a little off-center.

Dinghy was a poodle-terrier-schnauzer mix. In other words, he was a silky snap poo, or a Schnoodle. Dinghy went with me everywhere without his leash. He went in and out of the dog door whenever he wanted, and would sit on the front curb to watch the kids come home from school. They would all say hello and pet him; he was in heaven.

I'd take him to the beach and when I went swimming in the ocean I would say "Dinghy, stay. Do not come in." I would start swimming out then turn around and there he was swimming out to me. He was so cute—a wave would

come and I'd think, oh my God he's going to drown.
course he didn't; he always came up through the wave,
dling toward me. I would swim to him and take him bac

He also went shopping with me; in those days it was Bu
ocks in Sherman Oaks, which had the swinging doors. On
day I was walking out and I looked around and didn't see
Dinghy. I turned around and there he was behind the swinging doors saying "Let me out! Don't leave me."

When I played tennis up at Janet Leigh's, Dinghy would
come watch us. He never came on to the court, he just sat
there and watched. When I was shooting *The Waltons* and
doing the interior, my dressing room was on the set. He'd sit
atop the dressing room steps and wait for me to finish. He
would never run onto the set.

On his first birthday I decided to give him a birthday
party. I invited all the dogs in the neighborhood and their
owners, which were the kids, to his party. They brought toys
for Dinghy; I had a cake and a birthday hat that he wore. I
forgot paper plates and napkins so I asked my Dear Donner
(I like to call Robert that or "Pa") to please run get some. So
he went down to the Hallmark store and asked the lady for
some napkins, birthday napkins and birthday paper plates.

She asked, "Is it a boy or a girl?"

"It's a boy," he told her.

"How old is the boy?" she inquired politely.

But when she asked, "What's his name?" and Donner said
"Dinghy," she turned about face and stormed off. She didn't
think that was very funny, but we sure did.

Me, Robert and of course, Dinghy.

I had Dinghy for eleven years until he committed suicide, yes suicide. I really believe that he did. He happened to have an enlarged heart and wasn't supposed to do any heavy running and had to eat a special diet. Well that didn't work for me or for him. Yes, I cut down on the running but I wanted him to be a dog. On a Wednesday he was supposed to go in for anal gland surgery which we were hesitant about because we were afraid that the anesthesiology might kill him. The Friday before that I was going in for a hemorrhoidectomy, and I know he sensed something wasn't right with himself or me.

Two days before I had my surgery I found him in the street, hit by a car! He never went out in the street in eleven years. It broke my heart. I got drunk out of my mind, buried him in the sweet yard next to the church next to apartment.

I have not had a dog since. Somehow about ten years later I got into cats or they got into me.

Here's how it happened. Thirty-five years ago when I got sober, my life was a bit of a mess, to say the least. My first year of sobriety was not easy. I had pretty much lost everything and I bottomed out in acting, in relationships—everything. To make ends meet, I took a roommate, worked as a hostess in a restaurant, and taught acting in my apartment two nights a week. And I played poker every other week.

Well, my roommate Jerry's ex-wife and daughter had a cat and they had to take in a roommate who was allergic to cats, so Jerry asked if I would allow him to take in the cat. I said, "On one condition—that you keep it in your room and you make sure you take her with you when you leave." He named her Zelda. She was a red ball of fur approximately ten months old and, of course, when he left, he didn't take her with him. Guess who got to keep her?

She was the first of many. The next one was Annie two years later; she adopted us. I have had a total of eight cats at one time. I rescued four kittens from beneath a house because the house was about to be tented for termites. They would have died! Of course I rescued them. So I guess you

all me the crazy cat lady. Now I have four, two are
r-outdoor cats and two are outdoor-only cats. I guess
they're gone, especially the indoor ones, I might just get
other dog.

Since I'm already old, I'll have to get an older dog but that
would be fine, too.

Oscar and
Wild Thing.

Blondie.

Watch Out for Swans

In April of 2018, I was invited to go to Marshfield, Missouri for the Cherry Blossom Festival. It was their fourteenth year. I was to be on two panels, one was about *The Waltons*, the other was a panel talking about my career and my dad's career.

I had no idea where I was going to stay. They flew me there, meaning Nicholas Inman who invited me. He was going to put me up in a bed-and-breakfast establishment. I'm so glad I don't get into expectation that much anymore because I had no thought about where I was going to stay, what it was going to be like, who was going to be there—I just went. I was blessed to have been put up at the Swan Song Inn, hostess and owner Cheri Colson was the best! (and yes, the

name got me and, of course, was hoping it wasn't goin...
my swan song! It almost was, though!).

Ten acres of beautiful green lushness. Quiet and priv...
with a lake and a huge full grown swan (notice I said swa...
singular), ducks, and chickens. We had fresh eggs in the
morning for breakfast. You can even fish in the lake. I did
not fish in the lake.

Also staying at the Swan Song Inn was Marion Ross, who
I fell in love with. She played the mother on *Happy Days*.
Marion was there to publicize her book *My Days Happy
and Otherwise* with her assistant/friend of twenty-six years,
Gwen Berohn, who I also fell in love with. These two were
incredibly bright, funny women.

On the second morning, before we were driven to where
the activities were being held, Marion, Gwen, and I walked
down toward the lake. When we were about ten feet away
from the water, we noticed that the swan was swimming
toward us.

He reached the bank, got out of the lake and was literally coming right at us. It felt like a linebacker was coming
to attack us! At that point Marion said, "Let's get the f*** out
of here!"

The three of us turned around and started running back
to the inn. We were laughing so hard we almost peed our
pants! The swan still pursued us with wings flapping and
making horrific sounds. We finally got to the front porch,
turned around . . . and there was the swan right at the foot of
the steps.

were still laughing but we looked at that guy—his
was Mister—and he was still flapping his wings at us.
yelled "Hey Mister, buzz off!" He ignored us of course,
.t didn't come any closer! Needless to say, swans can be
.eally scary!

Don't be fooled by this tranquil photo of Mister!

The last night I was there, the event was having a closing
dinner but I just didn't feel like going. I was exhausted from
the last several days. Always being on, doing the panels, sign-
ing autographs and meeting people. I know it sounds like a
complaint, but I loved it, and I loved the people. *The Waltons*
fans are the best. They are very family-orientated.

I skipped the dinner and wonderfully I had the inn to
myself, well almost. I got my water and walked down to the

lake. I noticed Mister at the other end of the lake so .
down to the opposite end, sat in a chair just about st
from the water. I closed my eyes and just took in deep re
ing breaths. It was lovely. Shortly I heard flapping right ne
to my chair.

Yep, it was MISTER! OH, MY GOD! The LINEBACKER
was back! I didn't panic. Well, inside I did. All I could think
was DON'T MOVE!

So I just watched him. He was so close, I could lean forward and touch him! He started preening. He cleaned under
his wings but he constantly stopped to check me out.

Right now all I can think is NO ONE AROUND! Everyone is going to come back and find my body strewn all around
the lake! Dead, bleeding, no eyes! Okay, TMI!

Well he suddenly hit my chair with his wing! That was it!
I yelled at him so loudly. I won't mention what I called him. I
got up and ran—I scared him! And I'm alive to tell you about
it! Swans are beautiful to watch, from a distance!

When I was on *The Waltons* panel with Michael Learned,
Judy Norton Taylor, Mary McDonough and Marcia Woolery,
one of the questions asked was how we got our parts on the
show. Everyone mentioned they read or tested for it. When it
came my turn, I just looked out at the audience and said very
loudly, "I slept with the actor!"

Of course everyone laughed, but I quickly followed up
with "He was my husband in real life." A lot of the fans didn't

ve were married in real life. Donner and I always loved
ing together, so I ended up doing *The Waltons* for five
sons, and my new name was Sissy Walker. Hmm, Cissy
Vellman, Sissy Walker . . . it worked for me!

Christmas and Easter at the Wellmans

At our house Christmas and Easter were storybook magical holidays.

The Christmas Eve tradition in our family began with Mom and Dad having their close friends over, usually the Fred MacMurrays, the John Paynes, the George Chandlers, and the Townsends. All of us, including the kids, would sing Christmas carols while Dad played the piano. Then we would hang our stockings over the fireplace and since I was number five of seven, I was one of the younger ones. The five of us—Pat, Billy, Kitty, Timmy, and I—were two years apart, and then another four years from me to my brother Mikey and another four years from Mikey to Maggie. The ones were sent to bed early on Christmas Eve.

Once we were upstairs and in our beds, Mom and D would go to work along with the older siblings. They broug the tree in from the garage and all the presents. They would decorate the tree, put the train underneath along with all the presents. When we got up in the morning first we would have to have a little breakfast.

Our living room was wonderfully warm and huge. We had sliding doors—the old wonderfully well-built wood ones—and during breakfast Dad would say, "Gee, I wonder if Santa came." He would then go into the living room, turn on the Christmas tree lights, start the train going underneath the tree, then come back say, "Gee, I just don't know if Santa came. I guess we'll have to see."

We would line up in order of youngest to oldest first, then Dad would slide open the doors to the living room and oh, my God, it was a magical sight! The lights on the tree, the sound of the train . . . we just looked with awe, smiled and giggled. We had to first get our stockings from hanging on the fireplace and see what we had—there was always some maple sugar. I always remember a maple sugar Santa Claus or maple sugar maple leaf being in our stockings. And the presents, oh my goodness—roller skates, a bicycle . . . it was just magical.

Mom and Dad would sit and watch us all open our presents. Then we would watch Mom and Dad open theirs so we could watch them react with delight, which they always did.

Thanksgiving 1975.
Maggie, Mike, me, Tim, Kitty, Billy, and Pat.
Dad passed away that December.

It was a very special time, with a lot of laughs! And even when we all became adults and married and had our own children, except me, we would always go over for Christmas Eve to decorate the tree, sing carols, and enjoy each other. How lucky was I!

It was similar at Easter. After church, Mom would make brunch and we would have an Easter egg hunt. Mom made fudge eggs, sooo good, and she'd also make butterflies out of dollar, five and ten-dollar bills, plus all the hard-boiled and candy eggs and hid them. When I was young it was such a joy, but I must say being an adult and watching all my nieces and nephews hunt was so much fun. Of course we'd help them find them, especially the little ones, and just lik.

at Christmas, the little ones would line up in order youngest first to go out in the yard to hunt. Special men. that Mom and Dad gave us all!

I loved it so much that I did a similar thing at my hon when I was married, for both my husbands. I hid all sorts of colored hard-boiled and candy eggs and special treats, and they both loved it.

Celebrity Softball Tournament in Hawaii with Dear Donner

Dear Donner was a wonderful softball pitcher. He played in a lot of celebrity games.

One time we were flown to Hawaii with some other celebrities for a charity celeb game. The celebrities were Clint Eastwood and his then-wife Maggie, Mike and Mary Lou Connors, Peter and Joanie Graves, Rob Reiner, Lee Majors with then-wife Farrah Fawcett. We were all good friends.

Donner was so funny on the flight over. He said if the plane goes down they will name every celeb on the plane and then it would say, "Also on the plane was Bob Donner

and wife." Just like co-starring. Farrah and I were the b.
I must say one of the nights some of us had a bit mor.
a *lot* more to drink. We were at dinner in a private ro
The Eastwoods, Connors, Graves, Lee and Farrah and us t.
Donners, we were all having a fun time, laughing and tellin;
stories. Clint at one point said, "I want to whisper a joke to
Maggie and then she whisper it to the next person and see
if it changed when it got to the end." Everyone thought it
was a fun idea, so he whispered in his wife Maggie's ear. He
finished and Mag was laughing so hard and said "I can't tell
that." It was, needless to say, risqué, no, dirty. Well, that was
that.

Meanwhile there were beautiful swans made out of butter
on the table. Mike Connors said, "Let's mate them," and he
proceeded to do just that. Well, maybe you had to be there,
but at the time and with the consumption of alcohol it was
super funny!

Dancing the night away with Mike Connors on trumpet and Peter Graves on clarinet.

My Merlin Olsen and Rams Story

In 1968, I introduced my then-husband Robert Donner, a wonderful actor, to director Andrew McLaglen, who cast him in the movie *The Undefeated* with John Wayne and Rock Hudson. Because Andrew was a friend and knew I was a dancer, he asked me to stage the dance numbers. Also in the film were Merlin Olsen and Roman Gabriel of the Los Angeles Rams.

I was, and am, an avid RAMS fan! We were all together on location for almost sixteen weeks in Durango, Mexico. It was really a wonderful time. I'm giving you this back story because Merlin Olsen at the time was on the board of The Multiple Sclerosis Society. In 1976 they were doing a major

fundraiser event and he asked me to stage dance n.
for them. As a female jock, I thought I had died and
to heaven. Well, dear sweet Merlin wanted me to stag
ten-minute dance number for the Rams.

I said "Merlin, you only want two or three minutes."

He said "No, let's make it ten minutes."

"Merlin, trust me," I said. "Two to three minutes is
sufficient." I kept trying to figure out what kind of number
to do for them and one Sunday at a Rams game, *That's
Entertainment* was playing at half time, and I realized it
worked perfectly for the number for them. The first time I
met with the players was down at Long Beach where they
trained.

I'll never forget it. Here was Merlin Olsen, Larry Brooks,
Cody Jones, Fred Dryer, Tom Mack, Jack Youngblood, Jim
Youngblood (forgive me, I've forgotten the other names),
all ready to meet me and see the number I had prepared for
them to rehearse. Well, I put on the music, I did the number
and they all looked at me and said, "Lady, we are never show-
ering for you again after practice," because they really had to
work out with me!

As the weeks went by, I kept going down to rehearse with
them after their games. Usually one or two of them would be
injured with a sore shoulder or a bad knee. As a result, I had
to keep changing the number.

One rehearsal day I'll never forget. I think it was Larry
Brooks who was whispering to one of the other players and

eard. "I sure wish she'd make up her mind with the
ber we're doing. She's constantly changing it."

I turned on him and said, "If you guys would stop injur-
g yourself I wouldn't have to constantly adjust the number.
You with a bad knee, I've got to change the number. You with
a bad shoulder, I got to change the movements. So if you guys
would just not injure yourself when you play, I wouldn't have
to change the number all the time."

I was pointing my finger in their faces. Remember I'm
five-foot-three. They are six-foot-plus, and when I finished
yelling Larry looked at me and said, "Watch out for the little
coach."

They were wonderful. It ended up being a Rockettes-type
of number. When we did the show they were dressed in tutus,
tights, tennis shoes, shirts with numbers on them. They were
fabulous, all a bunch of hams.

Kicking it up with the Rams.

I almost didn't make it to the performance at th. erly Wilshire because I was fortunate enough to be sho a film called *FM* in Texas. But I took my gown and gorge leather and fox long coat just in case I got time off to fly in r it. Dear sweet director John Alonso got me finished in tim. to take a plane to see the Rams dance.

Well, I have to tell you I felt so special when I walked into the ballroom and all the guys saw me, they ran to me, they put me up on their shoulders. They were so happy to see me and I felt really special! The show was fabulous, as were they! When it was over I took the limo back to the airport. The flight was delayed due to weather, which scared me quite a bit. I did not want to be late for filming, especially since the director was so sweet to let me go.

The plane finally departed and yes, we arrived in Texas just on time! I looked like a hooker, having had a bad night wearing the same clothes I left in. The gown, the coat, and my hair a mess, makeup smeared from being on the plane trying to sleep. When I arrived at the hotel, the crew was just coming out to leave for location and they started pitching nickels and dimes and quarters at me, all with great senses of humor, treating me like a lady of the night, and not a successful one.

My Last
Howard Hawks Story

When I was eighteen, I met with Howard to test for the part of the Tomboy in *Red Line 7000*. He had already tested Laura Devon for the role and showed me her test. He really liked her. So that night at home I mentioned this to my dad. He recommended that I go to Howard and say that I just want to work with you—is there another role I can do?

As I said, Howard really likes Laura Devon. Well that probably was a big mistake because I would have had a great piece of film for my career, but on the good side I got to work with Howard, and I staged the dance number in the film.

And we became great friends.

One day while we were breaking for lunch, a bunch of

us were sitting around on the set; that was Laura .
Gail Hire, and Marianna Hill. The stage door opened
in walked Howard Hawks and another man. The girls m.
tioned that the other man was Howard Koch who happen
to be the head of the studio, Paramount.

I didn't think I knew him, I just knew who he was. Well
the girls said "Cissy, it looks like they're talking about you."

Oh, my God, all I could think was that they'd seen the
dailies and I'm fired! Needless to say, my self esteem was
lacking. Howard Hawks called my name and asked me to
come over. Again, I'm thinking, oh, my God.

I went over and Howard introduced me to Howard
Koch saying that Howard Koch wanted to meet me. Howard Koch looked at me and said, "I really enjoyed being your
babysitter on *Across the Wide Missouri*. I was your dad's third
assistant director on the film. I had my son Howard Junior
with me and he played with you and your brother Tim."
Again, oh my God! Well, interestingly enough, Howard Koch
and I became good friends. He was kind, generous and a gentleman. I adored him. His son Hawk and I have become good
friends and, like his dad, he is a very kind caring gentleman
and no, I didn't get fired.

My Richard Brooks– Jean Simmons Story

First off, I'm a good tennis player, or should I say I was a very good tennis player. I was asked to play tennis with Jean Simmons at her house. Oh, my God, I loved Jean Simmons as an actress. To get to know her as a person was quite exciting but I had to be on my best behavior because on the tennis court I can have a foul mouth.

We were playing mixed doubles and I was against her. I had missed a couple of shots and said "Damn, drat," instead of swearing. Well she proceeded to say, "On this court, you can say . . ." and she proceeded to say every swear word you can imagine in that beautiful English accent. It didn't

sound like swearing, it sounded so elegant. Well, I fell
knees and I just said, "I think I just fell in love with you.

She invited me to come play on the weekend with
guys. She said, "I think you'll fit in." Well, I arrived and wh.
an array of tennis players. Jean and I were the only womer.
but the men players were Gene Kelly, Alan Bergman, Conrad
Hall, Robert Webber, Robert Loggia—and Richard Brooks.

I get shy and quiet around people I don't know, so I was
shy and quiet and just watched tennis. When it was Richard
Brooks' time to play he looked at me and said, "Hey kid, you
come play with me."

About Richard Brooks's reputation—he was known to be
a yeller, screamer, ranter, and raver! YIKES! Well, we played
together. He missed some shots, I missed some shots. One
time when I missed one, he yelled at me, saying "Jesus, kid,
play the game. Get the ball!"

Without a pause I yelled back, "Hey, I'm playing my
game, why don't you play yours?" Oh, my God—I quickly
realized what I had said! I looked over to Jean but she just
grinned. Then I looked at Richard and he was grinning too.

He said "I think I'm going to like you kid." It was a test
that I passed. For years every weekend I played tennis at the
Brooks's and on Saturday nights Richard always showed a
movie in his screening room with the tennis group and their
spouses, dates or friends.

That's where I met Marlyn Bergman. Alan and Marlyn,
besides being the most prolific songwriters ever, were the
sweetest most down-to-earth people. I was a major fan of

films. He wrote and directed them. *Blackboard Jun-* *Cold Blood*, *The Professionals*, *Elmer Gantry*, *Cat on a Roof* and *Bite the Bullet* and many more.

I wanted to get Brooks and my dad together. So one Saturday I was able to invite Dad and Mom over to watch the tennis and stay for supper and a film. It was a glorious meeting. They were both so respectful of each other's films and the stories were incredible. At one point Jean said "I wish we had this meeting filmed."

Richard fell in love with my dad and vice versa. My father had never won an Oscar for directing. Yes he was nominated many times, and did win an Oscar for writing the original *Star is Born*. Richard Brooks found that unacceptable so he was responsible for my dad getting the D.W. Griffith Award for his achievements. Thank you, sweet Richard.

By the way, my favorites of my father's films are *Roxy Hart* with Ginger Rogers (*Chicago* was based on this film), *The Great Man's Lady* with Joel McCrea and Barbara Stanwyck, *Lady of Burlesque* with Barbara Stanwyck, *Beau Geste* with Gary Cooper, Robert Preston, and Ray Milland, *Goodbye My Lady* with Brandon DeWild and a Basenji dog (we ended up with two of those incredible dogs and if you're not familiar with them they are barkless), and *Island in the Sky* with John Wayne.

I was also blessed to have been on the location of Brooks's *Bite The Bullet* that my husband Robert Donner was in. Richard loved my husband's work and yes, they became good friends also. The location was in Chama, New Mexico and

most of us stayed in cabins near a stream. Richard lov
cooking, or should I say we both LOVED garlic, and Ri
had the only cabin with a kitchen. So I was the designa
cook. Everything with garlic and a lot of raw cloves.

With only a week left of filming, one night Donner an
I drove Richard out to dinner. I had driven to Chama in my
husband's Porsche, so Donner was driving, I was in the middle and Brooks in the passenger seat—it was very tight—and
at one point Brooks said, "I have to figure out who I want to
win the race!" Oh my God, that's the end of the film. Well he
did figure it out, a perfect ending too—it was a tie!

For my parents' fortieth wedding anniversary we, the kids,
did a surprise party for them, and invited all the people we
thought they would like to see. Well I have to say it was really
getting people Dad hadn't seen in a long time and cared
about. I got Brooks and Jean to come, and James Cagney, plus
there were so many good old friends there. Two years later
dad died.

Richard Brooks was a major influence on me. He made
me question my beliefs and politics, and I thank him for it
always!

I miss him. I miss my dad and I miss my surrogate dad,
Howard Hawks. Boy I was blessed to have had them and I
always have the memories.

Lovingly together, Dad and Mom.
By the way, Mom made that dress herself.

Top: *The Disorderly Orderly* stock company. Robert Donner and my brother Bill are standing on the far right. Me sitting on the floor with a cigarette.

Right: Brother Bill and me on *The Disorderly Orderly*.

Jerry Lewis

I met Robert Donner in 1963 on the movie *The Disorderly Orderly* with Jerry Lewis.

Now about Jerry Lewis. He was so much fun to work with, and I learned so much about comedy from him.

Jerry was also directing the movie and when he was shooting my close-up he would do everything in his power to make me crack me up. He'd make faces! So, I learned to stare at his left ear and also to clench my fists so my nails would go into my palms so I wouldn't laugh.

Jerry also taught me a big lesson about colors I should wear as a redhead (an orange-yellow redhead). I should never wear white or pale colors, he told me, but just stick with the dark blues and greens, and rust colors, and also black. That way my hair would stand out.

After the filming he invited me to join him in Ve[...] watch his shows. He wanted me to see the difference betw[...] the early show audience and the late show audience. E[...] there was such a major difference! The late show had a[...] the hecklers. How Jerry handled them was very funny and[...] educating.

In between the shows a group of us went to the Tropicana Lounge because Jerry wanted to tape record a new comedian there named Don Rickles. He wanted to sneak in—he did not want Rickles to know he was there—and while we waited to go in, Jerry played Blackjack with hundred-dollar chips. I was just watching.

At one point he looked at me and said "Here, play with these. I've got to go to the men's room."

Well he put in my hand approximately ten chips, $1,000 worth! I was getting paid about $500 a week. Needless to say, I just held those chips until he came back.

I said "Jerry, here take these. This is two weeks of my pay!"

Also Don Rickles was so funny and of course attacked Jerry in his inimitable way. I was so grateful to have been a part of all that.

Thank you, Jerry Lewis.

Paul Newman

My husband, Robert Donner, was cast in the movie *Cool Hand Luke* which was shooting on location in Stockton, California, in 1966. It had the most incredible cast, including Paul Newman, George Kennedy, Strother Martin, Jo van Fleet and even dear Ralph Waite, who later played the father on *The Waltons*.

They were on location for approximately ten weeks and I was there for most of it. The first day I arrived, my husband, dear Donner, took me into the dining room to meet Paul Newman who was having dinner with the director Stuart Rosenberg. At the time Paul was mixing his own salad with his own hands and when I was introduced to him he looked up with those incredible blue eyes—and in person, to be honest, well, there's just no description, he is gorgeous,

drop dead gorgeous—and he said, "Sorry about the har
can't shake hands."

I just looked at him and said, "I'll shake your hand I.
that anyway," and he giggled.

Well yes, being up there for as long as I was, I got to know
everybody in the cast and crew and we all became pretty
close. It was really interesting because all the actors who
were playing the guards sort of hung out together and all the
actors who were playing the prisoners hung out together. It
just sort of happened that way, and it was really very interesting to watch.

Some of the other actors had their wives with them, too. I
especially remember Strother Martin and his wife Helen. She
taught me a lot about how to make a long time at a location
feel more like home. Helen would buy colorful towels, plants,
rugs and some paintings. After that, I did that on all the loca-
tions I went on.

Paul was really a very quiet kind of guy, but so easy to
be around. You never felt he was a STAR! He was just one
of the guys. He treated everyone the same. There was also a
feeling during the filming that they were making something
special . . . everyone just felt it! And boy was that true. A
classic film!

Paul's wife, Joanne Woodward, would come and visit and
stay a few days at a time. Well, she was so easy to get to know
and so down-to-earth you felt like you'd known her all your
life. What a very special lady she is and what a special relationship they had.

A few months after the movie wrapped, there was the tribute dinner to James Cagney at the Beverly Hilton Hotel. Dear Donner was again on location on another movie so I went alone and joined the table of my mom and dad and my brother Bill and his wife Flossie. I must admit I looked phenomenal—I was wearing one of the dresses my mother had made for herself. It was a coral chiffon spaghetti-strap gown, tight on the bodice to the top of the hips and then had individual coral chiffon scarves that went almost to the floor. It was the kind of dress that you could picture Ginger Rogers wearing when she danced with Fred Astaire, and yes, I got a lot of attention with it. At one point I had to go to the restroom and the ladies and men's rooms were side-by-side, just off the lobby. When I came out, coming out of the men's room at the same time was Paul Newman. We started up a conversation, just like old friends catching up. He asked me how Donner was, and I told him that he was on location. I asked about Joanne and he said, "She's at the table, come over and say hello, she'd love to see you." So we both went back to our respective tables.

A couple of weeks later, one of the gossip magazines ran a picture of Paul and me side by side. It was obviously taken the night of the Cagney AFI dinner when we were coming out of the men's and ladies rooms. The caption said it was Paul Newman with unidentified woman! Gee, I wonder how Hollywood rumors start?

Two Wonderful Men

B ack to Dear Donner. I was twenty and he was thirty-one. I was not attracted to him at first, but we were on *The Disorderly Orderly* for eight weeks and we fell in major like! We were together constantly.

And yes, fell in love.

Dear Donner, as I call him, was very very funny, a wonderful comedian and one of the main things that attracts me to anybody is a sense of humor and he had a marvelous sense of humor.

I helped him with his career. I introduced him to Andrew McLaglen who also fell in love with him as a person and actor. They did at least six films together and remained good friends.

I also introduced him to Howard Hawks. He did two

films with Howard and they also remained friends. La
not least, Richard Brooks while we played tennis for a
years and Donner did *Bite the Bullet* with Brooks.

Donner and I used to laugh when we bought our hom.
We'd say the house was from McLaglen and the swimming
pool was from Hawks.

We never had children and we were inseparable. We
did everything together. We worked together on *The Waltons*, did stand up comedy together, played tennis and golf
together. We were married for fifteen years and the reason
our marriage ended was because of me. He loved me more
than anything and yes, I loved him, but I had a communica-
tion problem an "ism" problem. I never knew how to ask for
what I wanted or needed and was so insecure and was always
looking for the rush of something new.

I left him twice for affairs, he always took me back. I
was so young. I didn't realize how special I had it with dear
Donner until it was too late. A lot of this had to do with my
alcoholism. As of this writing in 2020, I'm thirty-five years
sober.

Donner is without a doubt one of the best men I've ever
known in my life. We remained friends and luckily for him
he married a wonderful woman, Jill Sherman, and she loved
him the way he should have been loved. Dear Donner passed
in 2006.

Do I wish I knew then what I know now? Absolutely.
Woulda coulda shoulda . . .

Robert asks me
to marry him on
location for *Rio Lobo*.

Greg and me
in celebration
mode.

My life today is really good though. Yes I remarried in 1987 to another good man, Greg Guydus. Greg passed in 2013. I was blessed to have met Greg when I was coming up on two years sober. At age forty-three I was wondering what I was going to do with my life. I had no husband, I had bottomed out on show biz, had a roommate, taught acting in my apartment, played poker once a week and was a hostess in a

restaurant just to make ends meet. Not a happy camper! I fel
that if this was it, I'm sober and hate my life, why am I living?

Thank God, I had many friends in AA who listened to me
crying over my life and who made suggestions. One was to
get into real estate, especially with all my contacts. I was fear-
ful that my brain wouldn't work anymore. Yet the program of
AA taught me to be willing! So I asked Perry, who suggested
I'd be great in real estate, where I should go to school for it.
He told me to go to Miller schools owned by Bob Miller and
Greg Guydus.

So I did. After a few days there, Mr. Guydus called me
into his office and asked me why I was there. I told him the
truth: I had no husband to take care of me, I needed to make
a living, and I didn't want a relationship. I had to find out that
I could make it on my own. Believe me, I would never have
said that if I was interested in having a relationship with him.
Who knew?

A few weeks later in the hall he stopped me and asked,
"How would you like to take the time to get to know someone new?" What a great, non-threatening line! He asked me
to join him after class the next night for dinner, which would
be around 11 pm. I told him not for dinner because I always
eat early, but I'd have a soda with him.

We talked for three-plus hours and that was that! I'll
never forget the date: January 28, 1986.

We were inseparable after that. He even came to AA to
watch me take my second year cake on February 16—he was
so very supportive of my sobriety! One year later we were

.rried. I learned through the twelve steps of AA and a
onderful caring sponsor to be able to commit to him. No
heating. Plus, he gave me the intimacy I so needed.

Donner was the love of my life, but Greg was my
special love. I married two really good men who loved me
completely. I'm grateful for it. Some people have said I should
find someone else. Are you kidding? No way! I had two great
men. And at my age, I'm selfish. I don't want to have to take
care of someone else. I did that with my sweet Greg who was
a diabetic with rheumatoid arthritis. The last sixteen years
were hard on the both of us. But he had the most incredible
positive attitude and sense of humor, even in his pain.

The first six years of our relationship we did everything
together. We played tennis, golf, and traveled. We were good
friends. Then his diseases really kicked in and fought each
other. Even walking was hard on his feet. Things change.
There is no guarantee in life. I learned to do things with
my friends, like walk Fryman Canyon several times a week
with my best friend Judy Farrell, a wonderful actress and
screenwriter.

We don't walk Fryman anymore, but Judy and I have been
friends for thirty-plus years. We still see each other weekly.
She knows everything about me and still loves me, as I do
her. After Greg passed and my grieving lessened, I got into
gratitude that we had twenty-eight years together and that he
is no longer in pain.

I'm a good loner, I have my home, pool, wonderful whim-
sical private front and back yards, two black cats, squirrels,

hummingbirds, and sometimes unwanted raccoons. I h
my AA program and my friends. I paint, love to read, p
poker on the computer (for free), and I have today.

I am blessed.

To sum it all up simply, I've had one hell of a life. And hope-
fully I will have many more stories to tell and a lot of more
years ahead of me to live them, one day at a time.

So I ask you, do I get my crown?

Acknowledgments

A great big thank you to my editor Nicole Gregory, a super lady who helped me keep going, book designer, Karen Richardson, my family, and especially to my beautiful sister Maggie Seven, who is the real writer, thank you for your love and honesty. People who have helped me be me: Jessica Overwise, AA members, Hannah Doberne, Didi Doheny, Judy Farrell, Maria Florio, Lori Lethin, Lynda Lyday, Charlotte Ray, Barrett Taylor, John Paul Coakly, Terri Weiss, my two Brit bookends Claire and Debi, Dr. Marty, all the Born to Act Players and their families, my two cats Mikey and Maggie, plus all my Sidney squirrels!

Photos are from my dad's file and my personal file except the photo of "Mister" by Jill Phillips, owner, His Fingerprint Photography, and the photo of me, the author, is by my New York buddy, actor/photographer Bob Knapp.

About the Author

Cissy Wellman, actress and dancer, was born Celia McCarthy Wellman, the fifth of seven children. She is the daughter of pioneer film director/producer/writer William A. Wellman, also known as Wild Bill Wellman, and Busby Berkely dancer and actor Dorothy Coonan. Raised in Brentwood, California, Cissy has appeared in more than forty TV shows and more than twenty films. She now lives in Valley Village, California. To find out more about Cissy, Google her name or look her up on IMDB.com

Made in the USA
Las Vegas, NV
08 March 2022

45237940R00067